# ANCIENT ITALY
## FROM ABOVE

WHITE STAR PUBLISHERS

# ANCIENT ITALY
## FROM ABOVE

**PHOTOGRAPHS**
Antonio Attini
Marcello Bertinetti

**TEXT**
Enrico Lavagno

## Contents

**4-5**  Hadrian's Villa, built between AD 120 and 136, at Tivoli (Rome), shows the Emperor's love of the Hellenistic world, which he knew very well, and his detachment from the models of architecture being proposed in Rome at that time.

**6-7**  Ostia (Rome), the city's main port until the 2nd century AD, is now to be found several miles from the coast due to the thousands of years of detritus deposited by the River Tiber.

**8**  At Paestum (Naples) in about 500 BC, the so-called "Temple of Ceres", more correctly known as that of Athena, was erected.

**9**  Pompeii (Naples) is a priceless testimony not only of the customs and habits of the time, but also of the complete topography of a Late Republican imperial city of that era.

**2-3**  Not only are the excavations at Pompeii undeniably lovely, but the site is known worldwide for the terrible tragedy that struck there on 24 August AD 79, which preserved the city virtually intact for history.

When the history of the 20th century is written in the future, it will include many records. The standard 100 years seem inadequate in order to embrace all the events that occurred, so much so that it was defined the "short century". In other words it is a time-frame containing more changes than in the entire span of the existence of human culture. Even as early as 1905, for better or for worse, on the crest of this wave, the two brilliant Wright Brothers of Ohio succeeded in launching a revolutionary new device onto the world market: the aircraft. It was the first means of transport that allowed human beings to observe their world and the way they transform it with sufficient clarity and stability.

The scope of such an invention was soon evident and has been applied to various fundamental fields, but the invention also offered some valid opportunities for discovery in contexts like archeology that were not vital. Early in the morning and toward evening, just before sunset, the light casts long shadows on the ground, as if a tomography of the territory were being performed. That is when invisible things come to light, fragile traces of lives lived, phantoms appearing in floating light, invisible from the ground but easy to identify from the sky. These are enormous round tumuli: roads and foundations of walls and columns, bridges, canals and basins, dating back 3,000, 2,000 or 1,000 years. Mere ruins that affect us simply because we all exist today only

thanks to, and because of, those who came before us: those who erected the tumuli, walls and columns, and above all, those who opened up the roads and canals.

From an archeological standpoint, Italy is one of the densest sites in the world. The scant territorial extension, its generic fertility and enviable climate have all conspired to create a complicated history for this peninsula, and in part this explains its wealth. From north to south, it is impossible to travel for even five miles without encountering some record of the past.

It is conceivable that you could travel the length and breadth of Italy, discovering some trace of each of the various periods, almost seamlessly connecting the Paleolithic to the present day. Nevertheless, too many signs tend to create confusion: too many different sites and contexts, when seen from the more extensive aerial perspective, further complicates the idea that is formed of archeological Italy. Moreover, given that those who initially settle into an area do so for very good reasons, almost all of the human constructions on this relatively restricted territory will be rebuilt in more or less the same place, time and again. The result is that each new structure covers its predecessor and conceals it, making them all the more difficult to comprehend. It is difficult to read Italy from the sky and to appreciate history as it deserves, but this is when the inventions of

**10** For its time (27 BC), the construction of the cupola on the Pantheon (Rome) was a futuristic exercise: a complex system of arches was used to discharge weight to the ground, with materials becoming increasingly lighter on approaching the summit.

the 20th century can lend a hand, partnering those of the 21st century, to offer crucial assistance in understanding.

Archeology, leaving behind that romantic image of adventurous quests for "lost things", now uses new tools, some innovative, some less so. Aerial prospecting falls into the second category: it is not particularly innovative, but comes up with some surprising results. Human passing, in fact, leaves immediately identifiable traces, enjoying a regularity that is unlikely to confuse. Many minor sites have been discovered during flight, both by simple observation and traditional photographic reconnaissance, and by the use of more sophisticated techniques, such as infrared photography.

A more refined instrument, now being extensively developed, is genetics, which reveals in swift succession even the remotest secrets of our past. The data and conclusions expressed by geneticists do not always concur, but this system makes it possible to establish many undisputed characteristics: the invisible traces of lives become visible, structured with the almost infallible precision of nature itself.

The travel diary that follows relates a discovery, in three phases. Both genetics and linguistics appear to precisely confirm the result. Beginning with the simple geographical criterion: north, center, south: it seems, in fact, that the peninsula is genetically divisible into equal strips of communities. The North with its Celtic (Liguria) and Venetian culture, is balanced by an Etruscan center, and

**12 left** The arena in Verona is one of the few amphitheaters of this size to have survived to modern times and, above all, it is still used for entertainment. It was built in the 1st century AD, with limestone blocks from Valpolicella.

in the South an Oscan (later Latin) substratum: the different dialect groups and the genes of today's populations, if compared to what we know of the ancient people, mark out three distinct regions.

Moreover, a surprising genetic "tradition" can be observed among these different groups of the Italian population, indicating that the countless invasions and colonizations to which the country was subjected have not made them so different from what they were thousands of years ago.

Nonetheless, we should not forget that the outline we have sketched out does not take precedents into account. For instance, the fact that the Celts were not the first inhabitants of Northern Italy, but that they replaced or merged with occupants who had arrived much earlier. Actually, Italy's populations rarely came via land, they came by sea. "From the Mediterranean to the coast then inland," summarized Sabatino Moscati. If this is true, the choice of a geographical itinerary along the peninsula encounters spontaneous confirmation in reality. If we start off from the northwest toward the South and the islands, we find at our starting point, that Valle d'Aosta had a megalithic culture, over 5,000 years ago of more or less the same age as the pyramids. And on reaching our last stop, it will be another megalithic culture, in Sardinia, that closes this millennial parenthesis covering a long stretch of prehistory and history.

In the middle we find Etruria, Rome, Samnia, Apulia, Magna Graecia, the Phoenician colonies, Campania (whose name has never changed) all marked by the signs, almost intact, of the Dark Ages that are still part of the journey. One example of many is Ravenna, with basilicas so incredibly similar to a Rome that is now vanished.

The fine climate and fertility were defining factors for making Italy an archeological universe dense with content, as previously mentioned. Ancient authors, not only the Italics, were very clear on this point: Italy is the most fortunate place in the world, at least in the world they knew. "Here it is always spring and the other months are summer; the stock enjoy a dual fertility and the trees are doubly fruitful," said Virgil. Varro echoed his thoughts, "You who have traveled in many countries, have you ever seen one cultivated better than Italy?" Dionysius of Halicarnassus said, "The loveliest thing (of all the marvels of Italy) is the climate, temperate in all seasons." Then Tacitus, "In all the world (...) the region that is the loveliest for the things that rightly take first place in nature, is Italy." Last of all, Strabo, "The coasts of Italy are, in general, without ports, but those it has are great and admirable."

Yet, by a natural counterbalance, an interminable era passed during which Italy was never that enticing. During the last Ice Age, which ended (or was merely interrupted, as many believe with good reason) 10,000 years ago, its blissful portrait was reduced to

**12 center** The small island surrounded by a swimming pool is the Maritime Theater of Hadrian's Villa at Tivoli (Rome), one of the Emperor's favorite refuges.

**12 right** Founded by the Greeks in 658 BC, Selinunte's name comes from the Greek word "sélinon", a typical wild fennel that grows in that area.

a pallid extension of deep, difficult forests that were almost impossible to colonize. It was the introduction of agriculture, presumably brought in from the Middle East about 7,000 years ago that made it possible to create stable nuclei, thanks to revolutionary ideas such as farming the territory. Only thus, in virtue of this greater stability and security, were the first "Italians" able to find the time and means to consolidate themselves, originating all the civilizations and cultures that we already know and we suspect, more that are still to be discovered.

In fact, it is surprising to observe how extensively the country's archeological panorama has developed in just a few years. Archeology, specializing in many branches thanks to the development of correlated fields, penetrates with increasing depth into ancient realities that were inevitably composed, like our own, of all that came before. Science plumbs the impenetrable, bypassing catastrophic volcanic eruptions, wars of destruction, deportations and the extinction of cultures. It has even begun to investigate the psychology of our forebears, slowly rebuilding it, reconstructing scenes from life and not just the ruins, as was formerly unavoidable. One quite unexpected consequence of all this is that concepts like "dead languages" or "vanished civilizations" lose credibility in the light of investigations and the results of reconstructive methodologies. This has the further effect of restoring to life the formerly dusty and yellowing matter of archeology and arousing the interest of the public: probably the most useful application of archeology in our times.

A fortuitous and interesting case even brought to light a flesh and blood patriarch for Italy: a quintessential person and personality. Flying over the Ötztal Alps, between Italy and Austria, we can see the point where the most ancient "Italian" ever known to us in his real physiognomy, the only person who has successfully crossed the ocean of time, was discovered. He lived such an intense life that we can almost see it through his eyes, thanks to virtual reconstructions of the Neolithic habitat of this Alpine region. From the dizzy "height" of 5,300 years ago, the Similaun Man, Ötzi, is old enough to have earned the right to greet those taking off to discover the secrets of a vanished world. Invisible yet present: right here below us.

**15**  Dedicated to the first bishop of Ravenna, the cemetery basilica of Sant'Apollinare in Classe, in the Byzantine style, was consecrated in AD 549. The circular belfry, dated about 9th century AD, is enriched by single, double and triple-mullioned windows.

**18-19**  The Forum in Rome, as in any other Roman town, was the heart of trade and judicial activities. Each building contained within was linked to the person who commissioned it which underscored it with an enduring political significance.

**20-21**  The Greek Theater of Taormina (Messina), built in the Hellenistic period (3rd century BC), was almost completely rebuilt by the Romans.

**22-23**  The Coliseum, inaugurated in AD 80 in Rome, comprised four sections and could hold 73,000 spectators: every bit as impressive as our modern stadiums built for the World Cup.

# Facts and figures about Italian archeological heritage

- Italy boasts the largest number of locations that have been declared UNESCO World Heritage Sites: 42 at the end of 2006.
- The total number of visitors to museums, monuments and archeological areas in Italy*: 33,048,137
- The total number of visitors to museums, monuments and archeological areas in Italy*:

  North    7,977,233

  Center   17,101,161

  South    7,969,743

- In 2005 the Coliseum-Palatine and Pompeii were the most visited archeological sites in Italy*.
- The top three regions in Italy for numbers of visitors were*:

  Latium            10,949,011

  Campania          6,463,951

  Emilia Romagna    5,452,701

- The gross revenue collected by the State for museum, monument and archeological area entrance fees was 93,971,161.98 Euros, almost double compared to 1996.

* Data from the 2005 report issued by the Ministry for Cultural Heritage and Activities. The data totals exclude Valle d'Aosta and Sicily, which are covered by special regulations for their Cultural Heritage departments.

**16** Alongside the Pompeii site, the Coliseum-Palatine is incredibly popular and is frequented by enthusiasts and tourists from all over the world. In the heart of Rome, the Imperial Forum site is a testimony to the past grandeur of the city known as "Caput Mundi".

# NORTHERN ITALY

Flying over the Alps is an intense experience. Not even flight lovers can predict what their emotions will be. Tall, unyielding mountains elicit a kind of sacred trepidation, while the depth of the valleys stirs the hypnotic anguish of the downward tug. Nevertheless, even a perspective with as little promise as this one can guide us through the past. We cannot know what emotions these places aroused in their first human inhabitants, but some clues suggest they were not unaffected by them; on the contrary, they were even more inspired by their surroundings than we are. The megalithic monuments brought to light in the Valle d'Aosta bear witness to the industry of the first *"Homines sapientes"* to arrive here. They scanned the skies, the moving stars, and the mountains in great detail and then positioned the biggest stones they could find in relation to all of these elements in order to perform rites, draw up calendars and commemorate their people. The valley is in effect an immense main road through the mountains and as such is the most auspicious place to advance into the chain, cross it and settle in order to exploit the territory and the trade flow. Which brings us to what remains of Roman Aosta, with the black walls and towers that have served the city unfailingly since the days when legions marched by on their way from Italy to Gaul. In 23 BC, Terentius Varro Murena founded a castrum here, under which Augustus was celebrated with a triumphal arch (this has been completely preserved under the peculiar slate roof). He also built a theater with an impressive surviving *scaenae frons* illuminated by arched windows, the Porta Pretoria gate and a bridge that is still in use, all built by 3,000 robust Praetorians. Looking eastwards it is possible to discern the underpinning that made the construction of such an important city feasible. At a short distance from the capital, appearing at intervals lies the remains of the famous Via delle Gallie, partly dug out of the rock (including an arch hollowed from granite and still served by bridges such as Saint Martin) it is a narrow arch over the Lys stream, standing steadfast for the last 2,000 years. Leaving the disquieting depths of the valleys behind, we encounter the more reassuring Val Padana landscape, the ancient panorama that has been molded since Neolithic times, beginning immediately after the glacier retreat. Lengthy human presence has witnessed nameless hunters-gatherers and primitive shepherds in action: pre-Celts, Ligurians, Celts, a smattering of Etruscans, Romans and various hordes of barbarians. However, practically all of the North's important archeological evidence dates back to the Roman

**24 left** Ravenna's basilica of San Vitale is one of the most beautiful examples of Early Christian architecture to survive today.

**24 right** The Aelia Galla Placidia Mausoleum (Ravenna) was erected in approximately the 5th century AD by the daughter of Theodosius as her final resting place.

**25** Dated to about the Augustan period, Turin's Porta Palatina is definitely the city's most important Roman Age monument.

**27** The remains of a Roman villa at Sirmione (Brescia), also known as the "Grotte di Catullo", are the most important testimony of a dwelling built in that time in Northern Italy.

era, with at least four important cities that still established their layouts on ancient grid systems. Turin, in this respect, offers an example on a metropolitan scale: the famous square street plan is based on what was imprinted on the city at the dawn of the Empire (late 1st century BC) and has been revived again and again over the centuries, as needed. Furthermore, the city successfully shows the Augustan remains, isolating them in vast, open spaces. As we fly over the center we see the outstanding Palazzo Madama, seeming so solitary between its two quite melancholy towers in the middle of Piazza Castello, and nearby the Porte Palatine gates, still striking as they loom alone in the great empty space that surrounds them. The respective polygon-based pairs of towers were part of the Porta Prin-

cipalis Sinixtra and the Praetoria, the ancient "façade" of that colony of 5,000 inhabitants. It was protected by 2526 x 2329 ft. (770 x 710 m) of walls, another 35 towers similar to those still standing, and an extremely beneficial urban structure, built to make best of the sunlight and prevailing winds. Exactly to the west of Turin, at the foot of mountains that may have witnessed Hannibal's marching army, Susa (Segusium) still has an Augustan arch set in the narrow valley bottom and one of its Roman gates, is called the Savoia. It is to the southeast, however, that one of the North's most spectacular sites can be found, little known and yet very visible from the sky. Libarna, in what is now southeast Piedmont, is in an area of ancient Gallic-Roman culture (the name of the town of Benevagienna maintains a refer-

**28 left** Aosta's Porta Praetoria gate was the eastern entrance to the city in Roman times. It has been perfectly preserved over the centuries and lacks only the marble facing.

ence to the Bagienni Gauls, the first to settle there around the 5th century BC). It can be identified from above thanks to the perfect circle of the 1st-century BC amphitheater, staring like a huge eye set in the plains, surrounded by hills. Bearing north, we soon encounter the River Po and beyond it the skyline of Milan, or Mediolanum, where the imperial seat remained for more than a century, impelled by 3rd-century AD crises, when Rome was but a shadow of her former self. It is in Brescia, further east however, that considerable traces of ancient Brixia can be seen from the sky – days when the city gleamed with monuments made from pure white Prealps limestone. Brixia was a great capital where Gallic and Roman culture merged at the end of the 3rd century BC, and where one of Northern Italy's brightest forums was built. The ruins of this forum are still visible from the sky, alongside its basilica, the theater and the *Capitolium*, a large ecumenical temple, consecrated to the gods of the Roman State religion and a local Celtic god. Brescia's fertile and beautiful surrounding area has always been favored by nature, particularly towards Lake Garda. If we head exactly to the east of the city, testimony of the Roman affection for these lands can be found in the villas at Desenzano and Sirmione. They are amazing both for their extremely panoramic positions and their elaborate architecture, comprising

hundreds of rooms for the fortunate residents and servants, panoramic terraces, covered walkways, huge gardens, baths and facilities supplied with spa waters, still in use today for thermal baths. Catullus lived what were possibly the happiest moments of his short life here, amidst this flourishing tranquility, and naturally he sang of its beauty in his verses. At the time when the Po Valley towns and villas prospered, from the 1st to the 3rd century AD, the territory was more densely wooded. It was scattered with as many farms and farmhouses, staging posts/inns and settlements as it is today, which revealed their importance through the monuments and villages situated at the junctions of the roads that originated in Via Postumia, connecting east and west. Flying over the road that has replaced the ancient route, beyond the Garda, Verona lies set in a beautiful loop of the River Adige, where it was likely to have been founded by the Romans in the Late Republic Age. Considering only what is clearly visible, the old city center boasts ten outstanding monuments. The Roman theater (1st century AD), not as famous worldwide as the amphitheater, is better known as the arena. It is set in such a panoramic position over the Adige and the old city that it appears even more striking. Of the walls, the slim proportions of Porta dei Leoni (1st century AD) survives, its pale stone far more graceful than

**28 center**  The Basilica of S. Apollinare in Classe, in Ravenna, is a splendid Italian Byzantine monument. Consecrated by Bishop Maximilian in AD 549, it still contains mosaics of rare beauty.

**28 right**  Rocca di Manerba, in the province of Salò (Brescia), owes its name to the cult of the goddess Minerva, who was worshipped there from time immemorial. During the Longobard period it was the site of a castle that was destroyed in AD 1787.

the squat Roman gates at Aosta and Turin. The arena, on the other hand, is an illustrious example of the ancient public buildings that have never ceased to be used: the arena continues to host audiences and performances, despite the loss of one order of arches and almost all of the outer walls. Nevertheless, viewed from the sky, the 44 concentric ovals of the tiered seats present a striking solidity, preserved thanks to a Renaissance restoration. Without diverting from the ancient *stratae romane* itinerary, we encounter a point, east of Verona, where the road that split the Po Valley (at that time Cisalpine Gaul) into two eastwards, the Postumia divides into two branches: one toward Greece, the other toward Pannonia. This is the site of Aquileia, which preserves conspicuous signs of its role as an important border city. It was founded in the Republican Age (2nd century BC) and prospered until the decline of the Empire. The forum is clearly visible from above, even though the columns of its encircling arcade are mere traces of what was once the heart of this great town. Traces remain of Republican and Imperial walls and other elements that were never lacking in a Roman town: baths, an amphitheater, basilica, terraces of houses and even an arena for chariot races. After all, in ancient times it was said that Aquileia was "sublime for its buildings", rich in public monuments and surrounded by villas. The city's vitality and fortune derived, however, from the river port, connected by the paved decuman from east to west. Remains

seen here include warehouses, shops and both private and state offices, and it was here that Aquileia's famous wares were transported: Baltic amber, processed metals, pottery and bricks, and, above all, valuable blown glass. The road to Rome from Aquileia hugged a coastline that is now set much further forward. The sea was closer but today as in the past, its course leads straight to Ravenna. The Empire retreated here before its fall, identifying the city with the magnificence that had typified Rome for 1,000 years. Ravenna's basilicas and the mausoleums of Galla Placidia and Theodoricus all remain intact and have been preserved for future generations the Late Roman architectural imprint. Ravenna, founded in the fabled time of the Trojan War (12th century BC) and inhabited by the Italic Umbri and by obscure Etruscan foreigners, was always important. Ravenna was the Roman fleet's port in the eastern Mediterranean from the times of Augustus (1st century BC – 1st century AD) and in the 5th century AD was the last capital of the Western World, then the seat of a Byzantine diocese whose importance is expressed in the powerful majesty of the basilicas of Sant'Apollinare Nuova and Sant'Apollinare in Classe, the church of San Vitale and the palace of Theodoricus himself. The leader of the Ostrogoths conquered the Empire and lost it shortly after. Ravenna is a dramatic snapshot of the end of an era and the birth of a new age. It is the perfect place to turn southwards and follow from the sky the still-visible tracks of a long-distant Italy.

**31** The Verona arena is one of the best-preserved amphitheaters surviving today. Built in the 1st century AD, it can seat 22,000 spectators and is still used for stunning opera performances during July and August.

**32** Aosta's Roman theater, built at the same time as the Verona arena, has a striking, austere 72-ft. (22 m) façade. Another feature of this monument is the cavea, which could seat up to 4,000 people and be covered securely in bad weather, as was the case in Pompeii.

**33** The Arch of Augustus, in Aosta, was built in 25 BC as a homage to Rome's first emperor, following victories over the native Salassi tribes. The single-fornix monument is 37 ft. (11.5 m) high.

**35** Porta Savoia in Susa (Turin), also called "Porta Paradiso", was erected in the 2nd century AD to defend the town from barbaric invasions. It has been modified many times, including the opening of the fornix, once much smaller, in order to ensure its closure, and a lowering of the towers in Napoleonic times.

**36 and 37** Turin's Roman Theater (left) and Porta Palatina (right) are some of the many traces of the period remaining in Turin or, as it was then called, Augusta Taurinorum (the Taurini were the tribe who lived in this area). The theater, with its 236-ft. (72 m) diameter, was not discovered until the late 19th century AD. The neighboring Porta Palatina (1st-2nd century AD) was used as a palace/fortress until the late Middle Ages. Many superstructures were added only to be removed later on during the restoration. Porta Palazzo's name (Palace Gate) derives from its function and is also used to indicate the adjoining area.

**38-39** Libarna, near Serravalle Scrivia (Alessandria), strategically positioned between the Po Valley and Liguria, owes its celebrity to famous 2nd-century BC Roman findings that provide valuable information on the structure of towns from that era. The amphitheater (above right) and the theater can be distinguished below the built-up area.

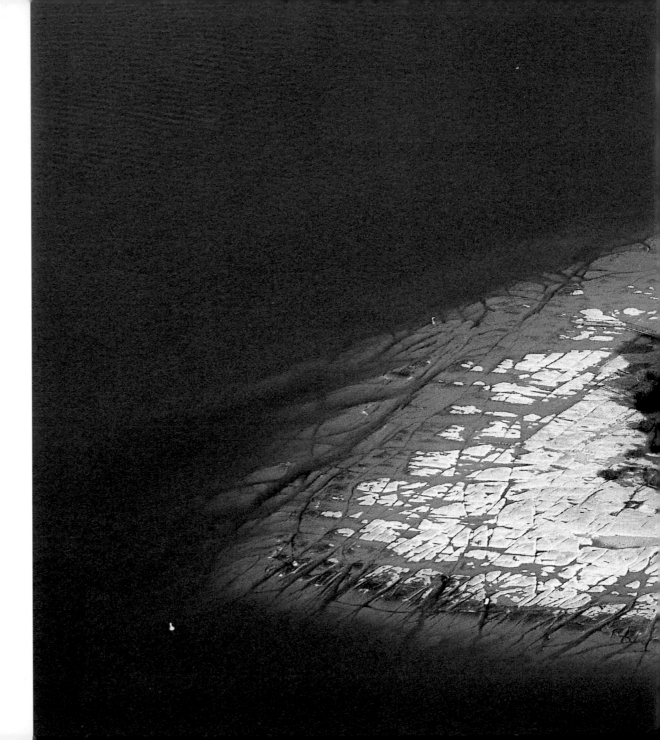

**40-41** The archeological area correctly called the "Grotte di Catullo", lies in a picturesque area of the Sirmione (Brescia) promontory. The complex comprises a Roman villa of the First Imperial Age and an antiquarium richly embellished with mosaic flooring, shops and a heated pool.

**42-43** Also featuring on Lake Garda, is the Manerba (Brescia) promontory, with a small peaceful town in an area called the Valtenesi. The park enclosing the fortress (built in the Middle Ages) is also outstanding for its nature.

**44, 45 and 46-47** The arena in Verona was built in the 1st century AD, between the reigns of Hadrian and Claudius, for both gladiator and wild animal performances (*munera gladiatoria* and *venationes*). Amongst the inscriptions found, one was left by Generosus, a *retiarius* (a gladiator who fought with a trident and a dagger) from Alexandria, Egypt, who fought here 27 times. The amphitheater staged events for the people and maintained this tradition in the Middle Ages, when it was used for jousts and tournaments. It is a considerable size: the axes respectively measure 500 and 400 ft. (152 and 122 m), including the "Ala" fortifications.

**48** The colony of Aquileia was founded in 181 BC, also to exploit the proximity of the Natisone-Torre river. Port facilities were built here, as well as a network of canals to regulate tidal flows. Vessels could also be towed upstream, hauled by ropes along paths marked out for that purpose, called the *viae helciariae*.

**49** Notwithstanding the difficulty of excavating the Aquileia area, due to the extensive phreatic waters present in the terrain, many buildings have been brought to light, including the forum area, burial grounds, dwellings and oratories.

**50 and 51** 1,500 years ago, the Basilica of Sant'Apollinare in Classe (Ravenna) was set on the sea. The Roman fleet was in fact stationed at Classe ("Classis" was the name of the military fleet). The church, which is now a UNESCO World Heritage Site (since 1996), is now a few miles from the Adriatic because of the River Po's inexorable silting.

**52-53** The mausoleum of Theodoricus was commissioned by the king of that name in AD 520, as his final resting place. The building is in Istrian stone, and the dome is now badly cracked, explained by a curious legend: Theodoricus had been told that he would be struck by lightning and killed, so he took refuge in his tomb (believing it to be impenetrable) each time there was a thunderstorm. However, the building was struck by lightning, which cracked it and killed him.

**54-55** The church of San Vitale in Ravenna is the sum total of all that was promulgated in Constantine's AD 313 edict. The classical forms show a great oriental-style influence. Initiated in AD 525, it was consecrated in AD 547, by which time the city had been under Byzantine domination for 7 years.

# CENTRAL ITALY

If the land stretching to the north of the Ligurian Apennines and that of the Tuscan-Emilian Apennines has been, for many centuries, a vast frontier much less populated than the sunny lands of the center and the South, we need only pass the watershed crest to find that the sites become more numerous. They are so evident that they give the impression that archeology is a science involved with current affairs. And thinking of the distant past of Tuscany, Emilia Romagna and Northern Latium, the first name that probably comes to mind is one of the most famous in history. The Etruscans are famed for being a mysterious population even though as we fly between Latium and Tuscany many places where their memory survives are very evident: for example Mantha (Mantua), Velathri (Volterra), Pupluna (Populonia), Sveama (Sovana), Tarchuna (Tarquinia), Kisra (Cerveteri) and, of course Ruma (Roma). From north to south, Volterra, Populonia and Cerveteri (from the 6th century BC onwards) are famous for their necropolises: cities built for the dead whose most fascinating aspect is that they are reproductions of the cities of the living. Tombs hollowed out of the subsoil in Volterra, carved out of the tufa hillsides of Populonia and So-

vana (as in Asia Minor: an important detail, as will become apparent) with thick circular walls and grass-roofed domes, or shaped like huge tufa cubes in Cerveteri. Kisra, in particular, is a city frozen in time, with strange labyrinthine "avenues" between the different tombs. The Etruscans – who called their houses "pera" and their tombs "suthi" – made each grave a replica of a dwelling. These were either elegant, many-roomed apartments or large, luxurious cabins: the tombs were square and those carved out of the rock imitated the former, and those on the circular bases, the latter. The Etruscans enchant each and every observer. Their origins, for example, have been the object of discussion since the times of Herodotus and today there are two schools of thought. The first surmises that they were immigrants who came to the Italian peninsula in about 900 BC. It is not known where they came from - from the Turkish coast impoverished by famine, as the rocky tombs would indeed confirm, or perhaps from Hungary, which would link them to tribes from distant times and places such as the Sami from what we now call Finland - or alternatively it is suggested that they had lived there since the beginning of time and had

**56 left**  Built in AD 315, to commemorate the victory of Emperor Constantine over Maxentius, the Arch of Constantine in Rome is the largest honorary arch to survive.

**56 right**  The Mausoleum of Cecilia Metella, on the Appia Antica in Rome, is the tomb built in about 50 BC for one of the city's most important and influential women. She was the daughter of the Consul Metellus and the wife of Marcus Licinius Crassus.

**57**  Rome's world-famous monument, the Coliseum, was used for gladiator exhibitions. There were two main entrances: the Triumphalis for the gladiators and the wild beasts, and the Libitinensis, used to dispose of corpses.

**59**  Originally, this was Rome's Porta Appia (so-called because it marked the beginning of the Appian Way, which was built to connect Capua and Brindisi). However, over the centuries, the name changed to Porta San Sebastiano, due to its vicinity to the catacombs, which are just over a mile away.

simply taken the best of various incoming cultures such as Phoenicia, Mycenaean Greece, Egypt and Mesopotamia. The most probable theory, however, gives credence to a legend because the story of Aeneas – a pilgrim-seafarer returning from a Troy razed to the ground and subsequently the founder of ancient Roman traditions – is more credible than Virgil himself thought. The seeds of a culture that came from far away brought by hunger or war, inseminated Ruma, instilling the city with tremendous drive. Etruscan supremacy was crushed by Roman might in the 4th century BC but not before they had voluntarily moved to Rome, or rather into Rome, cohabiting with the Latin residents who knew neither riches nor social differences. The Etruscans infused the city and its inhabitants with advanced techniques, rituals and a judiciary - a cultural force. Rome, for its part, added to the development process a potentiality that the Etruscans lacked: the capacity to combine different ethnic groups (the seven hills symbolize this quality), to mix them, reorganize them and, on a fundamentally egalitarian basis, invest them with responsibility within a political system in order to activate them for a common purpose. Continuing south from Cerveteri, we find the site of what was to be the last Etruscan city-state, the powerful Veio (Veie in Etruscan). Here a 7th-century BC tomb has come to light, that of a Rasenna prince who lived during this period of his people's greatest splendor. The exceptionally lavish tomb, with a large chamber measuring 15 x 15 ft. (4.5 x 4.5 m), was a reproduction of the prince's home when he

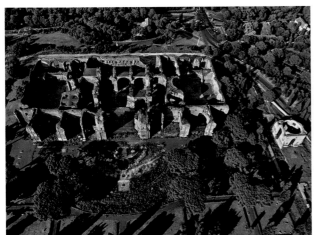

**60 left** Caracalla's Baths (Rome) were built by Septimius Severus and inaugurated in 216 AD, during the reign of his son Marcus Aurelius Antoninus Bassianus, known as Caracalla (from the name of a hooded Gallic tunic that he often wore).

was alive and contained his ashes, together with the bones of his family. After this important person had been buried, many other members of the Rasenna family were interred close by. Veio was the last place where the Etruscans were able to reign in their own name. In the 4th century BC Rome destroyed it with such zeal that they left no visible traces. However, just 12 miles south, it was Rome itself that absorbed the Etruscan legacy and prospered. It is likely that billions of people have visited the Italian capital from that time to the present, and although everybody may have heard of Rome and innumerable people have walked round it, far fewer have seen it from the sky. There is little point in listing everything that the city has to offer in terms of archeological evidence: for a few fortunate centuries this was the capital of the world. And even if it was not the megalopolis, with more than a million inhabitants, that is often suggested accurate estimates reduce that figure by half, which does not in any way diminish the historical importance of the city. It was the small and large towns that gravitated around it, as well as the thousands of foreigners who flooded in every day, that made it immense. The Trajan markets, the equivalent of an ancient shopping mall, were visited by a profusion of Numidians, Thracians, Syrians, Persians, Germans, Greeks and Gauls. They were also frequented by the Latin and Ital-

ic people who strove to be "at home" in this multitude. The markets were built with an extensive use of bricks and marble, with two or three floors of shops set around an enormous central hall. The Trajan and Antonino columns, whose marble was sculpted from top to bottom with 3-dimensional figures, tell of the lives of conquests, splendor and poverty that the Romans lived. The events are narrated through the eyes of the Britons, the Hyperboreans of central Asia and perhaps even the Seri, the "silk men", as the Chinese merchants and observers of the powerful Han dynasty (2nd century BC-2nd century AD) were known. Flying over Rome enables us to see the dome of the Pantheon (1st century BC-3rd century AD) which was for centuries the biggest in the world. It was certainly one of the most futuristic of all time, built in the 2nd century AD with light materials and an ingenious technique to prevent it from collapsing. Indeed, Roman archeology does not only offer us the sad ruins of roofless palaces and districts, but instead, whole public buildings which, in general, have been saved because the power that had belonged to the pagan empire was transferred there. In the Middle Ages the Pantheon itself was not demolished with the intention of building something else with the stone. It had been converted into a Christian church, just like the Baths of Diocletian (4th century AD), which retain

**60 center**   The deviation of the course of the Tiber in AD 1575 stripped Ostia, the ancient Roman river port, of all its defensive value thus transforming it into a quiet little town. The excavations that revealed the Roman ruins were started in the AD 1800s, under Pius VII and Pius IX.

**60 right**   The Fortuna Primigenia sanctuary, in Palestrina (Rome), dates back to the 2nd century BC and had three orders. The upper story was absorbed into the Palazzo Barberini, which today houses the National Archeological Museum.

their original appearance in full and are identical to when they were built for the welfare of his people, by then in decline, by one of the last real emperors of the pre-Christian West. Regaining height over Rome while bearing sharply to the west, we shortly reach a point directly above what was once the port to the capital of the world. In just a few minutes we cover a distance that would have taken a day or more to transport Egyptian obelisks, tigers from India, exotic birds to give to friends for dinner or even slaves from dozens of different nationalities. Even though it was one of the liveliest sea ports that could possibly be imagined, Ostia maintains the square plan of military encampments because it was built in the 4th century BC as the garrison defending the mouth (ostium) of the Tiber and the salt pans behind. In those times the salt pans were almost as valuable as a gold mine (for a long period the legionaries were paid in salt, hence the word "salary"). Incidentally, the rational organization of the large warehouses - which stored Egyptian grain, markets, competitive commercial offices, temples, baths and condominiums of three or four floors housing the people of Ostia - probably helped to organize an unbelievable traffic volume of both vehicles and people … unlike Rome, which was unbearable. Ostia was modern and efficient and attractive, but it was a port of merchants, workers and shopkeepers, various cult followers and prostitutes. It was most certainly not the home of a divinity, which can be found, however, by turning east, more or less equidistant from the capital. Tivoli is famous for Hadrian's Villa (2nd century AD), so enormous that it would have been difficult for another private home to compete. The wise emperor built it with a singular lack of restraint and it contained theaters, temples, a library, large and small spa baths and pools. It was very much like a decentralized and safer Rome. The complex also included a police barracks, because Hadrian knew that his power and his life were as uncertain as the most humble of his legionaries. All around the capital, following a path of concentric rings, we find that the sites of the city-states that Rome encompassed as it grew are not easily visible from the sky, but their names confirm the value of tradition as a tool serving historiographers. Ante Amnes, Ardea, Collatia, Crustumerium and Lavinium, for example, are cities that until now had only been mentioned in legends, including the narration of an incident that was absolutely fundamental for the survival of primitive Rome: the Rape of the Sabine Women. Archeological research (done without excavations but instead through an intuitive study of sources and an on-the-spot survey) has made it possible to establish that obscure Sabine strongholds, impregnated with the Greek culture that was highly-rated by the Romans, were found exactly where the legend said they would be.

**63** The realization of the Trajan Markets complex (left in the photograph) presumably began between AD 94 and 95 during Domitian's Empire. The Forum of Augustus (right) stands on a rectangular area 410 x 393 ft. (125 x 120 m) in size. Along one side there was a temple dedicated to Mars Ultor, where the Roman Senate met when it had to make war decisions.

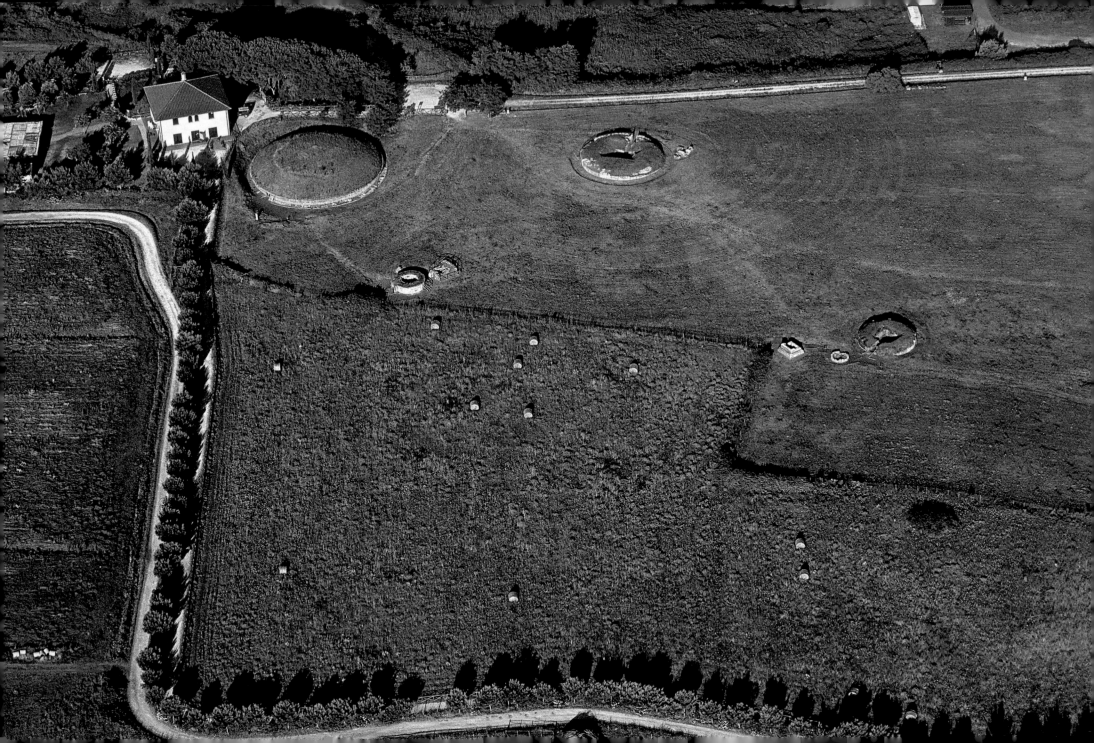

**64** Around the Gulf of Baratti (Livorno), the archeological remains of the Etruscan period are now celebrated by the Baratti-Populonia Nature and Archeology Park. The tombs visible in the photograph are part of the Podere San Cerbone necropolis. The circular tomb is also called the Cart Tomb due to the two vehicles that were found inside, which now reside in Florence National Archeological Museum.

**66** The Tomb of the Funeral Beds, also in the Podere San Cerbone necropolis (Livorno), was discovered in AD 1897 by the archeologist Isidoro Falchi. This monumental grave is of the burial mound type and spans more than 65 ft. (20 m) in diameter.

**67** Between the 5th and 6th centuries BC, the Etruscan city of Pupluna (now known as Populonia, in the province of Leghorn) became the Mediterranean's most important iron-making center: hematite, a ferric mineral extracted on the island of Elba, was processed there. The industrial center was set outside the city walls, on the Poggio della Porcareccia, and has now been partially excavated.

**68** The ruins of the greatest Etruscan temple at the top of the eastern hill of Tarquinia (Viterbo), known as Pian della Regina. The Ara della Regina Temple has always been very visible and consequently was the object of pillaging over the centuries. It was probably dedicated to the Etruscan goddess Artumes, the counterpart of the Greek goddess Artemis and the Roman goddess Diana.

**69 and 70-71** The necropolis of Cerveteria, which is about 30 miles from Rome, became a UNESCO World Heritage site in 1994. The Etruscan tombs are set in a ring around the ancient dwelling that dates back to the 9th century BC.

**72 and 73 left** There are many Roman remains in Spello (Perugia) testifying to its economic importance during the Augustan period. These include the oblong fortification belt that was then absorbed as the base of the medieval boundaries (photograph page 72) and the amphitheater ruins outside the urban center (on page 73, left).

**73 right** It was likely that the construction of the apse of the church of Sant'Agata eclipsed the Roman theater in Spoleto. Built in the 1st century AD, it was refurbished almost immediately and, over the course of the centuries, finally absorbed by the surrounding buildings. It was brought back to light in 1954 and since then has hosted the Festival dei Due Mondi (Two Worlds Festival).

**75** The Roman theater of Gubbio (Perugia) dates back to the 1st century AD, as do many in Italy, and expresses the importance of the town during that period. With its lavish mosaics and inscriptions it is still a summer venue for classical performances.

**76** Villa Adriana in Tivoli (Rome) was ordered by the Emperor Hadrian, who had it built on land belonging to his wife Sabina. He was probably seeking to reproduce the architectural beauty that he had seen during his travels. In the foreground is the Pecile, a huge rectangular quadriporticus used as a wrestling school and which was the site of a garden with a central fountain.

**78 left** The building containing the fishpond at Villa Adriana in Tivoli (Rome) was part of the Winter Palace and was the emperor's private residence.

**78 right** The so-called Piazza d'Oro (Golden Square) in Tivoli owed its name to the sumptuous furnishings, systematically plundered and pillaged from AD 1500 onwards. It was probably the Emperor's summer triclinium.

**79** The Villa Adriana Canope, ending in a pavilion, is a pool built to commemorate the canal that went from Alessandria to the city of the same name on the Nile, famous for its magnificent night celebrations.

**80** The Maritime Theater at Villa Adriana in Tivoli (Rome) was probably a place to which the Emperor liked to retreat from the world. At the time of its construction, the central island was linked to the rest of the building by two wooden swing bridges (now in set in stone and unmoving). Hadrian liked to retreat here and swim in the circular canal as it was inaccessible from outside.

**82-83** Today's Palestrina (Rome) is built on the ruins of the ancient town of Preneste (said to have been founded by Ulysses) which was much loved by the Roman nobles. One particular attraction was the temple dedicated to the goddess Fortuna Primigenia. This is the building over which the Barberini family built their palace and it is now a museum.

**84 and 85** The villa of Tiberius at Sperlonga (Rome) had belonged to his mother Livia, who originated from the area. It was extended and embellished by the emperor. Apart from the building itself, which was brought back to light in the 1950s, the villa is famous for a natural cave on its land that overlooks the sea and is encircled by the villa, like a natural theater. Statues of rare beauty were found in this cave, at the center of an expanse of water where banquets were held on artificial platforms during the summer. At the entrance of the cave there was also a deep fishpond, which provided the ingredients for special Imperial meals.

**86 and 87** The Temple of Jupiter Anxur, probably built between the 2nd and 1st centuries BC, stands at the top of Mount Sant'Angelo in Terracina (Rome). Alongside the building, to the east, there is a sort of square plinth, with an opening that allowed the Temple priests to reach a cave. Then to the west we can see the Piccolo Tempio (small temple) which was used for civil purposes.

**88 and 89** Ostia Antica, a few miles from Rome, was the capital's old port. After centuries of abandonment, partly due to malaria, which was rampant, the site now allows visitors to enjoy experiences similar to those offered by Pompeii. In both photographs we see the Museum (the pink building near the river) and the Capitolium (the building with the front staircase). The latter was the town's main place of worship and was built in about AD 120. Today it is only a shadow of its former self: the construction boasted a facing of African marble which has been systematically plundered since the Middle Ages.

**90** The Theater of Ostia (Rome) was built in 12 BC, during the Empire of Augustus. Subsequently, during AD 196, it was extended, given the city's ongoing expansion of the city, and reached a capacity of 3,500-4,000. Even the orchestra pit was modified to accommodate the Late Imperial fashion for water games.

**91** On the right of the Ostia Antica Museum we see the Casa di Diana, a "condominium" which unusually reached 65 ft. (20 m) in height and had three or four floors. In Ostia the *insulae* (the quarters of the lower and middle classes) comprised apartments. These differed from those of Pompeii, which extended in width but not in height. This was perhaps due to the massive development of the town when the Trajan port was built between AD 130 and 140.

**92** The Marciana Spa in Ostia (Rome) was right in the suburbs, by the seashore and was named after Trajan's sister, Marciana, whose bust was found during the excavations. The very fine mosaics that were found depict athletes at prize-giving ceremonies and probably decorated a changing-room floor.

**93** The first gate encountered on arriving in Ostia Antica (Rome) from the sea was the mighty Porta Marina, which suffered the most attacks and damage from enemies. The quarter immediately outside remained active even in the Late Ancient period (about AD 380).

**94** Along Rome's Appia Antica we find the spectacular Circus of Maxentius, 1,683 by 300 ft. (513 x 92 m). The terraces could hold up to 10,000 spectators and the Circus was used for chariot races. We can still glimpse the starting box *(carceres)* for the 12 chariots participating in races.

**95** The tomb of Cecilia Metella, the wife of Crassus, lies along the Appia Antica. The battlements which are visible today were built in about AD 1299 by the noble Caetani family who occupied the tomb and incorporated it into a fortified castle.

**96-97** One of the most marvelous achievements of Roman civilization was the construction of aqueducts to meet the city's ever-increasing need for drinking water. The arches visible in the photograph are near Rome. They were forced to built them (AD 312) as a solution for the problem of well water, which was no longer sufficient for a city that was continuously expanding.

**98-99** At one time the old Porta Appia, today Porta San Sebastiano, must have been an impressive sight for any wayfarer entering Rome. The building, which has lost an arch (for safety reasons) is now the Museo delle Mura Aureliane. It is also possible to visit part of the wall as far as the Porta Ardeatina.

**101** Rome's Piramide Cestia is the funeral monument of Caius Cestius, who died in 12 BC. During his lifetime he had been one of the seven *Epulones* involved in organizing banquets in honor of the gods. The pyramid, notwithstanding the considerable dimensions, was built in just 330 days. Immediately behind, we can admire the Porta San Paolo, at one time known as the Porta Ostiensis, also part of the Aurelian walls.

**102-103** In Rome's Centocelle suburb there are some very well-preserved remains of the aqueduct built between AD 222 and 235, by order of the Emperor Alexander Severus

**104 and 105** The Tiberina isle lies in the waters of the Tiber, in the center of Rome. In ancient times it was the home of the temple of Esculapius, the Greek god of medicine. Over the centuries it has maintained this tradition and subsequently became the site of a Franciscan isolation hospital; today it houses the Israelitico hospital. After the Second World War the upstream part of the island was completely rebuilt, including the Fatebenefratelli hospital. The two bridges which link the island to the mainland are the Cestio (on the left of the photograph) and the Fabricio. On the southern tip it is possible to see the Emilio or "broken" bridge.

**106** For once the Coliseum and the Arch of Constantine, in Rome, are in the background of a photograph. Here we see the archeological remains on the Palatine. From bottom left, moving upwards: the Domus Severiana, the Palatine Stadium and the Domus Augustana. At the back, to the right, lies the Basilica of Maxentius.

**108** The Roman Forum, for many centuries the heart of the Empire's political life, was a muddy swamp when the city was founded among the Palatine, Capitoline, Viminal and Quirinal hills. The construction of the great Cloaca Massima sewer allowed drainage and reclamation of the area. Its vicinity to the Forum Boarium marketplace favored its enhancement and consecration in about the 7th century BC, as a political, administrative and judiciary hub of the city.

**110** It is rare to find Roman monuments that are more famous and immortalized than Rome's Coliseum and the Imperial Forums. In this photograph we can identify the Temple of the Vestals, with its arcades and pools - most likely containing fountains - and the Temple of the Dioscuri, although only three columns on the eastern side remain. The temple was devised by the dictator Aulus Postumius Albinus, who had dreamed of the Dioscuri intent on watering their horses at the Giuturna fountain situated close by, after his victory at the battle of Lake Regillo.

**111** The Arch of Septimius Severus, situated in the northeast area of the Forum, was dedicated by the Senate to the Emperor Septimius and his two children, following their victory over the Parthians in AD 195.

**112 and 113** The Basilica of Maxentius and Constantine (the great arches at the top of the photograph on page 112) was built in about the 4th century, on the ruins of the Temple of Peace. It was completed by Emperor Constantine, who mounted an enormous statue of himself within. The church is that of Santa Francesca Romana, formerly Santa Maria Nova al Foro Romano, where the 14th-century saint was buried. Alongside is the Arch of Titus and in the background, the Coliseum dominates the scene.

**114** At the edge of the Roman Forum area we see (top left) the Arch of Septimius Severus, the 16th-century church of Santi Luca and Martina and the Curia, the seat of the Senate. It would appear that the latter was founded by Tullus Hostilius, even if its current appearance is due to Diocletian's restoration following the fire of AD 283.

**117** The Emperor Trajan and his works are the protagonists of this photograph, which shows the markets named after the great emperor (identified by the semicircular structure in the center) and crossed by the Via Alessandrina, the Forum and the famous column of the same name. The Forum, which is bigger than the Imperial Forums, was built by the architect Apollodorus of Damascus, who began it in AD 107. At the center there was a bronze equestrian statue of the Emperor. The spirit of exaltation of the greatness and accomplishment of Trajan is reflected in the column bearing his name, which narrates the commander's exploits against the Dacians. In AD 1587 the statue of Trajan mounted on the column was replaced by one of St Peter

**118-119** The construction of Trajan's marketplace began, according to some brick inscriptions, between AD 94 and 95. The building technique is in the "masonry" style, comprising a cement structure covered with bricks. The whole structure exploited the slope of the hillside, excavated as per the designs for the construction of the Trajan Forum by Apollodorus of Damascus.

**120 and 121** The Forum of Augustus, even though incomplete, was inaugurated by the Emperor on 1 August, 2 BC. Everything about it had to be a celebration of the foundation of Rome and of the gens Iulia, the city's new founding family, into which Octavian had been adopted. In the northern portico, there was a giant statue of the Emperor dedicated to his genius: it was 35-40 ft. (11-12 m) high with hands were an incredible 4 ft. (1 m) in length.

**122** Rome's Domus Aurea was built by order of Nero, after the terrible fire that destroyed the city in AD 64. Today, of the 150 original rooms, only the core of the Colle Oppio building remains and is 1300 ft. (396 m) in length.

**123** The church of Santa Francesca Romana in Rome was built in the area of the Temple of Venus, and lies between the Arch of Titus (left of the photograph) and the Arch of Constantine. Set against the Temple is the Forum Antiquarium. Only certain parts can be visited at the moment.

**124-125** As with many of the better-preserved Roman monuments, the Temple of Antoninus and Faustina (left) in the Forum, avoided becoming an open quarry thanks to the fact that it was converted to a church (San Lorenzo in Miranda, built between the 6th and 8th centuries AD). The elegant circular building on the right, is known as the Temple of Romulus, but it is possible that the title is wrongly attributed. In fact, many experts do not consider it a place consecrated to Rome's legendary first king, or even to Romulus the son of Maxentius, but think that it is a temple for Jupiter or the household gods.

Classical period, we find an inscription with which Benedict XIV (Pope from AD 1740 to 1758) prohibited further plundering of the amphitheater. The monument was completely covered in travertine, which was used to embellish many noble Roman palaces.

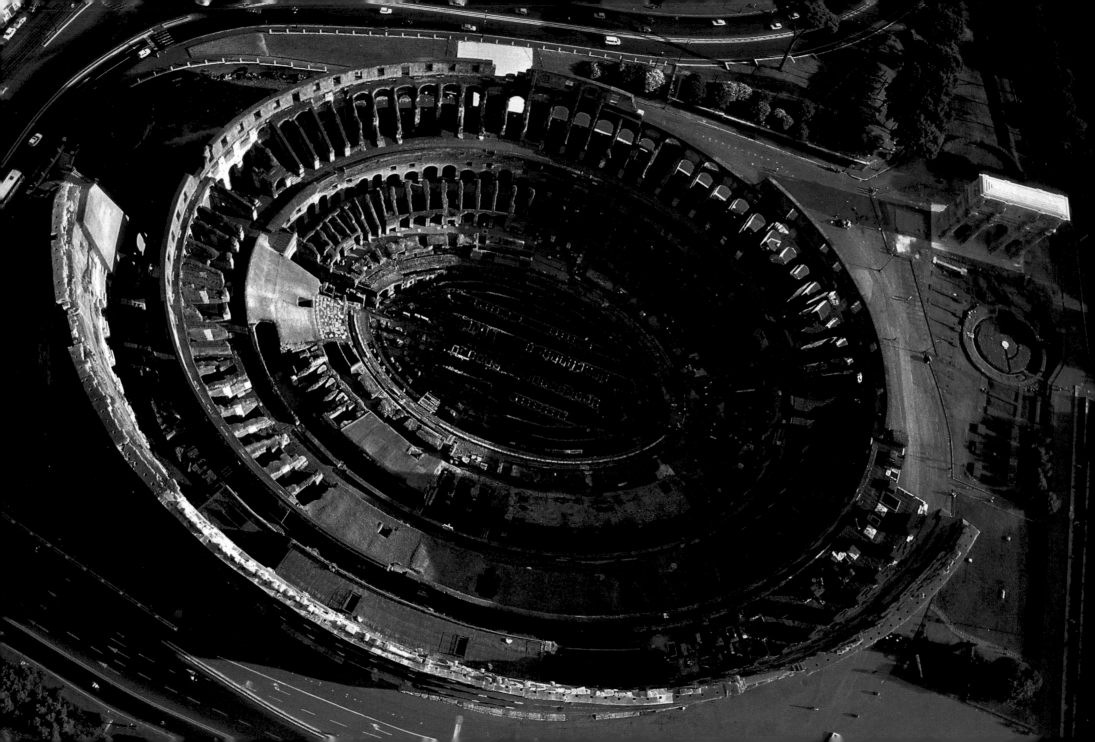

**128 and 129 left and right** The Coliseum had four tiers making a total height of 170 ft. (52 m). The main axis of the elliptical structure is 840 ft. (256 m) and the minor is 615 ft. (187 m). On the top floor we can see the hollows where the beams rested, supporting the canopy that protected spectators from sun and rain. This "awning" was then anchored to the ground with ropes fixed to marble posts, now lost.

**130-131** Underneath the Coliseum arena there were numerous passageways and chambers used by the gladiators (sick bays, temporary lodging, canteens) and to cage wild animals. There was also a lift and ramp system for moving the unfortunate contestants directly into the arena. Entrance into the Coliseum was free and Romans would queue from the night before. The amphitheater could hold 70,000 spectators, accommodated on the terraces according to social status.

**132-133** Rome's Palatine Hill preserves the oldest of the city's memories: it is here that we find the house said to have belonged to Romulus, who founded Rome in 754 BC. In the photograph we see, left to right, the Domus Flavia, the Domus Augustana and the Palatine Stadium.

**134** The Domus Augustana, built on Rome's Palatine Hill, was the Emperor's private residence from the time of Domitian onwards. Its beauty and grandeur are due not only to its embellishments and restoration, but also because it was never abandoned. The Domus Flavia was, on the other hand, the ceremonial palace.

**135** The Circus Maximus, the biggest entertainment building ever built, was continuously enlarged and embellished after its construction during the reign of Tarquinius Priscus. The Circus was used mainly for chariot races and especially for the Roman or "Great Games", the equivalent of the Panhellenic Olympics.

**136** The Palatine Stadium (top) and the Domus Severiana (bottom) are in the very heart of the oldest part of Rome. The former was built by Domitian, even though its typical oval boundary walls dates back to Theodoricus. The Domus Severiana was built by order of Septimius Severus as an extension of the nearby Domus Augustana and was fitted with its own central-heating system.

**137** The Temple of Vesta, with its characteristic circular plan, stands next to the Ponte Palatino bridge (top left) and is unchanged since the time of Septimius Severus. The holy flame of Vesta was kept alight here, tended by the Vestal Virgins, who resided in the building behind. In the top right we can see the small Temple of Fortuna Virilis, and in the foreground at the bottom is the bell tower of the church of Santa Maria in Cosmedin.

**138** Castel Sant'Angelo, built in AD 139 as a mausoleum for Emperor Hadrian and subsequently used as a fortress and papal prison, owes its name to the statue of Michael the Archangel installed on its roof. The Ponte Sant'Angelo Bridge, over the Tiber (right), was built to link the building to the Campo Marzio. In the 17th century the statues of ten angels were made and added by Bernini.

**139** Set in a garden of cypresses, lies the Mausoleum of Augustus (also containing the ashes of his family members), the Via del Corso and the Tiber. Near it are the Ara Pacis, the church of San Rocco and other colonnaded buildings built during the Fascist era.

**141** Castel Sant'Angelo is one of the most famous monuments in Rome and owes its name to Pope Gregory the Great. During the plague of AD 590 the Pope had a vision of an angel sheathing its sword, and the large bronze statue atop the monument commemorates this vision. In this detail we can distinguish the different phases of construction of the building: the cylindrical base is of Hadrian's mausoleum, the walls and upper part were added in the Middle Ages for the popes, and the garden was installed in the 20th century.

**142** The construction of the Theater of Marcellus was begun by Julius Caesar and finally completed in 17 BC; the theater was dedicated to the Emperor's nephew. It was subsequently subjected to structural changes until, in the 16th century AD, a palace was built. The latter is still there, primarily as the property of the Savelli family, then subsequently acquired by the Orsini family. The lower part, which is the Roman structure, was excavated and restored in the AD 1930s.

**143** The great dome with its central opening, makes the Pantheon unmistakable. The temple, built from 27 BC by Marcus Vipsanius Agrippa, was rebuilt by Hadrian and in AD 609 was converted into a Christian church. Today the monument houses several tombs of the Savoia royal family and that of Raphael Sanzio.

**144 and 145** The Diocletian Baths complex, a stone's throw from Termini railway station, was begun in AD 298 by the Emperor Maximilian in honor of his fellow Emperor, Diocletian. It was completed about eight years later, between May AD 305 and July AD 306. Over time, the majestic building became a store for building materials, but it retained part of its marble decoration right up until the 15th and 16th centuries. In the 16th century the whole baths building was converted into the Basilica of Madonna degli Angeli, attached to the Carthusian monastery. Today it houses the collections and restoration workshops of the Museo Nazionale di Roma.

**147** The great cloister of the Carthusian monastery of Santa Maria degli Angeli is known as "Michelangelo's cloister" because tradition attributes it to a design by Buonarroti. The great artist was indeed entrusted with the conversion of the Diocletian Baths, commissioned by Pius IV with the Papal Bull of 27 July AD 1561.

**148** The impressive Caracalla Baths, built between AD 212 and 217, were in working order until the end of the 6th century AD, when the discontinuation of the aqueducts rendered them unusable. It is interesting to note that the finest example of Imperial baths ever built required the creation of the Acqua Antoniniana, a special branch of the Acqua Marcia waterworks. The great chamber in the foreground at the center of the image, is all that remains of one of the "palaestrae" located in the baths.

**150-151** A vast panoramic shot shows the grandeur of the overall Caracalla Baths complex. Archeological reconstructions indicate that the vast surviving building - built on a square plan, with sides over 1,000 ft. (305 m) long - although a giant structure was, in reality, only the central part. The Baths were set in their own gardens, surrounded by an enclosure and with a raised promenade, of which a small section has survived the ravages of time and can be seen at the bottom right of the photograph.

# SOUTHERN ITALY

In the mists of time humans arrived somewhere in the South. 800,000 years ago early humans installed a camp near to what is now known as Isernia. The place was safe, with lavish grasslands and few tall trees, so the hunters lingered for hundreds of centuries, thus beginning the story of the Homo genus on the Italian peninsula. From Isernia, flying directly south, as the Gulf of Naples comes into sight, we reach Capua, called *Capue* by the Etruscans, who founded the settlement in about 600 BC. They developed it over three centuries into an influential city, the third most important in the Western Mediterranean. Then it betrayed Rome to side with Hannibal and Rome eventually overwhelmed it. In fact, the most striking monument and the most visible from the sky, is Roman: the Campano amphitheater, with a 40,000 capacity, second in size only to the Coliseum and probably the model for it. In any case, all of the important towns in Campania Felix seem to have been competing to have the biggest amphitheater: if we continue south, the distance from Capua to Pozzuoli is short. We find the location of the Roman world's third largest amphitheater, built to seat 20,000 plus spectators and still the ancient town's most striking monument. Yet it is the territory's geological torment to have given Pozzuoli its most extraordinary feature, as well as its fame as a seaside and spa resort. The

elegant market with cipolin marble columns, subsided to below sea level but subsequently emerged and disappeared several times over the centuries, at the whim of the interminable bradyseisms. From Pozzuoli, the town where "Justice rules" (Dicaearchia for the Greeks, who founded it in the 6th century), we bear a sharp east and the route takes us to the foot of the volcano, where we notice the oval of another famous amphitheater, closed for 10 years, in AD 59, after a mortal brawl amongst gladiator fight fans. It is difficult to describe Pompeii, Stabia, Herculaneum, Pozzuoli or Baia because they are the only places in the world that were encapsulated, just as they were and handed down to history. Yet lively Pompeii had existed for over 1,000 years from when the native Oscans had established the first nucleus of huts. It was later transformed into a city by the Greeks, Etruscans and Samnites between the 7th and 4th centuries BC. Given its excellent geographical and environmental position Pompeii was always a cosmopolitan center, one that the Romans adored. Its end is renowned: it is possible that some 3,600 people died there between 24th-25th August AD 79, as the city disappeared under a blanket of ashes at 800° C. Continuing the flight southeast, past Punta Campanella and the island of Capri where Tiberius built his outrageously lovely villa, we see the Gulf of Salerno curving around

**152 left**  The Dioscuri Temple's remains are the tourist icon of the city of Agrigento. The temple was dedicated to the twins Castor and Pollux, the sons of Zeus.

**152 right**  Famous as a basilica, the Temple of Hera - the bride of Zeus and main divinity of Poseidonia - is one of Paestum's three great Doric temples.

**153**  The Temple of Segesta, built in the 5th century BC, in pure Doric style, was never completed. Nonetheless, it is defined as one of the most beautiful in antiquity.

**155**  The theater of Siracusa was built in the 5th century BC, then rebuilt in the 3rd century and finally completely remodeled in the Roman era.

Paestum. Isolated on the Sele plain, ancient Poseidonia is even more daunting, with its giant Doric temples. Founded in the 7th century BC by the Greeks from wealthy Sibari in Calabria, a cultured people - lovers of wit and banquets, Poseidonia became the most astonishing example of the Magna Graecia style. The temples, seen from above, cast titanic shadows across the flood plain during the 6th and 4th centuries BC. They were severe and indestructible which was also thanks to the "anti seismic" qualities of the alluvial land. The Roman town, with its amphitheater, forum and walls stretches to the east and the north. Here our route doubles back and we head north, where Trajan's triumphal arch (or Porta Aurea, AD 114), the best-preserved of all in antiquity, announces that we are in Beneventum. This

Samnite city, the enemy of Rome, came under its control in the 3rd century BC. In the 1st century AD Trajan chose it as a transit point for the Via Appia Traiana in the direction of Brindisi, a port of vital importance for the survival and expansion of the Empire. Bearing northeast, towards the Gargano, we catch an impressive view of Lucera and its Angevin walls. It was founded by the native Daunia people, but the name is Etruscan and is thought to mean "sacred woods", "light of Ceres" or "town of the Luceri tribe". Lucera was a faithful ally of Rome against the Samnites. It is built with all the buildings facing the center so as to offer the least resistance to the winds. Further over, to the southeast, Venosa was founded by pre-Hellenic settlers, taken by the Samnites in the 7th century BC and, lastly, in

**156 left** The Capuano amphitheater, second only to the Coliseum in size, is the most important Roman building found in the Campanian town of Santa Maria Capua Vetere, built on what was once the site of Capua ("the other Rome," as Cicero defined it).

the 4th century was transformed by Rome into a colony. In the 1st century BC, when the poet Horace was born there, Venosa was one of Italy's major cities and the conspicuous ruins of the archeological area confirm this fact. It is a short distance from here to the sea where we find ancient Egnatia, south of Bari, whose history dates back to the 15th century BC. It began life as a simple group of huts, but its favorable trade position for the opposite shore of the Adriatic meant that it was always an important port. The Roman ruins survive, including significant traces of the Via Traiana, the amphitheater and the forum, but there are also relics of the massive walls built by the native Messapii in the 8th century BC. Without losing sight of the sea, moving down to the southeast, we reach Lecce, another Messapian city (5th century BC) with the Roman name of Lupiae. In the Imperial Age the city had a great economic boom and it became an important trade and transit location. Invaded by barbarians in the 6th century AD, it fell into decline but, unlike many other Roman cities that never recovered, Lecce flourished once more under the Byzantines who turned it into an important center of Greek culture. Turning our backs on the sea and heading southeast we cut diagonally across Calabria to Sibari (founded in 720 BC), Crotone (708 BC), and Locri (673 BC), which were the main Greek colonies along this coast of Magna Graecia. Inland, however, we find the places settled by the people that are extremely special for the history of the peninsula: the

Ithaloi, a peaceful group known as cattle breeders, lived deep in Calabria long before the Greeks arrived. Then, in the 8th century BC, they began to be influenced by and eventually were absorbed into the greater panorama of Magna Graecia and Rome. Yet their name lives on to designate what is now a nation. Passing Cosenza, beyond the Aeolian Islands and across the Tyrrhenian sea, Segesta stands in the far west of Sicily. It was founded by the Elimians, one of Sicily's three native peoples, already present prior to the arrival of the Greeks and Phoenicians. The city was not a Greek colony, but became Greek to the point that its great Doric temple became one of the best examples of the Classical style, even if the god to whom it was dedicated is not known to us, being local rather than Greek. Selinunte, almost exactly to the south, past the Montagna Grande which at 2,463 ft. (750 m) looms over Segesta, was founded in the 7th century BC by Greek settlers. It was one of Sicily's loveliest and most powerful cities, yet it has remained in ruins since the 4th century BC, when the Carthaginians destroyed it completely. Nevertheless the city of "wild parsley", as its name indicated, is still striking with a vast section of the built-up area and eight main temples still clearly visible and again, it is dedicated to gods (in this case Greek) that we do not know. Agrigento, known to the Greeks as Akragas, stands on a great spur, east-southeast. It was a city that boasted possibly 200,000 inhabitants at the peak of its fortunes in the 5th century BC. Once

**156 center** Pompeii is the most evocative archaeological site in the world. In the image we can identify the Via del Foro, with the arches of Caligula and Tiberius.

**156 right** The Roman theater of Sessa Aurunca in the Caserta region is set on a hillside in a panoramic position facing the Gulf of Gaeta.

the dangerous Carthaginians were overwhelmed, the city extended to the Valley of the Temples. Today the temples are the same color as the land and the rock, an almost coralline ochre, because this was what they were built with, but at the time they must have been completely covered in paint of very bright shades. The Concordia Temple, is the most well-proportioned and best-preserved example from the Hellenic era. To the east, on the Ionian coast, ancient Syrakousai was founded in 733 BC, by Corinthian Greeks. The city immediately found fortune and prospered, but it was subsequently repressed by tyrants for many centuries until Rome liberated it in 214 BC. The first hint that we are reaching Siracusa from the east is the sight of an impressive plateau fortress. The Eurialo ("nail head") Castle, with its three moats and great stone walls, is the world's best example of a Greek fortress. The Castle was founded in the 4th century BC by the tyrant Dionysus, 200 years before the city became Roman. And then the Romans left the other monument that is so clearly visible from the sky: the amphitheater, larger than that of Pompeii (century AD) and 460 ft. (140 m) long. Before crossing northeast in the direction of Sardinia, back over the Tyrrhenian sea, we meet Taormina, which retains the position of ancient Tauromenion. It was founded in the 4th century BC by Greek exiles and its theater (3rd century BC) which looks south towards Etna and the Ionian coast is set in one of the most enchanting scenarios in the world. Leaving the Strait of Messina to the right and proceeding northeast, the first dry land we meet is Sardinia. From the 9th century BC the Phoenicians installed large numbers of warehouses here, both on the coast and inland. They were more merchants than conquerors, but they appear not to have integrated very well with the indigenous population, who had been on the island for seven centuries. In fact, about 30 miles southeast of the Phoenician merchant port of Tharros, the megalithic village of Su Nuraxi seems a precursor to medieval castles, with its massive central tower reinforced by further peripheral towers and surrounded by a maze of circular dwellings set one against the other. The layout speaks of an early urban development phase, similar to what was happening in Campania and Latium, and the first Sardinians may have used these unique "fortresses" as meeting places, religious sites or seats of authority. The last Nuraghi, dating back to the centuries BC are, however, surrounded by walls that can be up to 10 ft. (3 m) thick which were evidently for defense. The people followed on as fathers and sons do, each absorbing, disturbing or wiping out their predecessors. These are normal events in the evolution of human history and, in fact, the ancient people of the Nuraghe were disturbed and absorbed by the interference of foreign presence – the Phoenicians, Greeks and Romans. Yet it is also true that on this island a surprising rate of genetic conservation still exists, as if hinting to the fact that that the population has not vanished, just as its castles have not vanished, and from the sky they tell us part of an ongoing story.

**159** The Nuragic complex of Su Nuraxi, the biggest in Sardinia, stands in a dominant position between the Marmilla and Sarcidano regions.

**161** Pozzuoli, in the province of Naples, is famous for its bradyseism phenomena, which affects the entire territory. However it is even more famous as it is the only city in the world to have two Roman amphitheaters. In the image here we see the Amphitheater of Flavius, built by Nero and seating 20,000 spectators. Unfortunately very little remains of the small amphitheater, which was cut in half in order to allow the passing of the Naples-Rome railway line in the early 20th century.

**162** The origins of Sessa Aurunca are extremely ancient. It was founded by the Aurunci, who called the settlement Suessa. Today's town is surrounded by medieval walls and circular towers. Sessa's theater was certainly one of the most refined of the Roman era: proof lies in the amount of marble and sculptures brought to light during excavations.

**163** Pozzuoli's Macellum is a unique and spectacular monument to the past commercial greatness of ancient Puteoli. It was an elegant market dating back to centuries AD, with a large and well-preserved arcade, three majestic cipolin marble columns (unfortunately, in the image they are hidden by protective scaffolding) and a circular tholos that once had a roof.

**164 and 165 left** The Capuano Amphitheater, also called the Campano Amphitheater, enjoyed many centuries of greatness. Its decline began with the barbarian invasions and the desertion of the old inhabited center of Capua. It was actually the people of Capua who plundered the town and used the recovered material to build the castle.

**165 right** The village of Santa Maria Capua Vetere was built on the site of an ancient cathedral: Santa Maria Maggiore. It was given the significant name of Capua Vetere when it became an independent municipality, emphasizing the historical continuity with old Capua and its remains, of which the amphitheater (easy to see in the image, besieged by the modern town) is the most famous monument.

**166** Cuma was the first colony built on the mainland of the Italian peninsula by the Greeks, in the 7th century BC. The Greek settlers probably came from the island of Pithecusa (Ischia), and subsequently founded Naples on the site of destroyed Partenope (in Greek the name "nea-polis" means "new city"). This is where the Sybil of Cuma, mentioned by Virgil in his Aeneid, lived and was closely linked to the worship of Apollo.

**167** Recently, in lower Cuma, the remains of an amphitheater were brought to light: a building dating back to the 2nd century BC and now partially in use as the foundations of several dwellings. In the ancient port area the remains of the sanctuary consecrated to Isis have also been found.

**168-169** This view takes in a part of Pompeii's archaeological site, allowing us to simultaneously appreciate an ample stretch of the Campanian plain, as far as Vesuvius. At the end of the Via dell'Abbondanza we can identify the majestic mass of the amphitheater (right) built in about 80 BC; unlike other similar constructions of the Imperial Age, there were no cellars under the arena, which was set much lower than the ground level of the square. Alongside the amphitheater, the enormous building we can see was the great palaestra (left), a gymnasium of the Imperial Age, built in a rectangular area surrounded by tall walls. In the background the unmistakable shadow of Vesuvius, whose AD 79 eruption destroyed Pompeii.

**170** From the sky we enjoy an extensive panorama of the archeological site, even though new Pompeii is encroaching fast. On the right we can clearly make out the amphitheater and the great palaestra; to the left, the area of theaters and the forums.

**171** Next to the Great Theater (left), dated to the first half of the 2nd century BC, there is a small roofed theater, the Odeion (or Small Theater, right), built for musical performances between 80 BC and 75 BC. Behind the cavea of the Great Theater we can note the large green square of the Samnite palaestra, surrounded by an elegant Doric arcade.

**173** The first real excavations in the area of Pompeii began in the 1700s, ordered by the Bourbon King, Carlo. Since then, methodical research has alternated with improvised excavations, often followed by pillaging and theft. Today we can appreciate Pompeii to its full extent, as presented in this image which was taken from the more or less vertical standpoint of Porta di Stabia. In the foreground we can see the theater district, with the lengthy Via Stabiana stretching down towards the Porta del Vesuvio gate (not in the image). The green rectangle that can be seen at the center of the image is that of the Terme Stabiane baths.

**174-175** The main street seen below, running horizontally, is Via dell'Abbondanza, one of the thoroughfares of ancient Pompeii, which leads into the Forum square (far left) and along which we will find some of the most famous buildings: the Casa di Eumachia (the green square to the left) and, at the junction with Via Stabiana, the Terme Stabiane baths (in the foreground, with the grassy courtyard and a portion of red roof). Via dell'Abbondanza still has its original paving and is complete with wide sidewalks.

**176** Here is another overview of the center of Pompeii, with the Forum and the most important buildings (Basilica, Macellum, Temples of Jupiter and Apollo, Casa di Eumachia) in the foreground below, and the great looming Vesuvius.

**177 left** Among the important buildings that overlook the Forum, we see the Basilica and the Temple of Apollo (in the image), the city's main religious building of very ancient origins. The sanctuary's current appearance dates back to about the 2nd century BC.

**177 right** Located at the junction between Via del Foro and Via degli Augustani, we find the Macellum, a large covered market with a central courtyard where fish was cleaned.

**178** Set at the heart of the town, the Forum was the political, religious and economic center of Pompeii. The great square was surrounded on three sides by arcades, and on the north side it was closed off by the Temple of Jupiter (Capitolium, top left) and two honorary arches.

**179** Adjacent to the Macellum (bottom right), a building of the Imperial period (left) featuring an apse has been identified as the Temple of the Public Lares: the divinities that protect the city. Above, beyond the Forum square, we note the Temple of Jupiter (right) and the Basilica (left).

**180** Pompeii's Villa dei Misteri is a splendid example of suburban villas. The villas were occasionally used by the owner, but more often than not, they were entrusted to a farmer (vilicus) who administered the entire estate. During the excavations numerous casts have been made of the unfortunate wretches taken by surprise and killed by the eruption in the servants rooms.

**181** The Casa di Venere, found near the amphitheater, owes its name to the fresco on the south wall depicting the goddess of beauty facing toward Pompeii, of which she was the patron. This dwelling is also an extremely luxurious suburban villa, with gardens and fountains, swimming pools and baths, statues, frescoes and mosaics: here the rich Roman aristocrats could enjoy some well-earned rest after working in the city.

**182** In the image we can see the Casa di Venere (top) and the Casa di Giulia Felice (lower down). The former is restrained in size, but the latter is undeniably huge. The complex is divided into two sections, with independent entrances: one section of the dwelling area, more full and decorated, was private whereas the other section, with the room set aside for the baths, was public. A major feature of this villa is the presence of a fishpond in the center of the garden, with a sort of grotto fashioned in the style precious to the god Pan.

**183** A view of the so-called regions I and IX, in the eastern sector of the city, highlighting the Via del Citarista, the house of the same name (foreground, left) and the Casa dei Quadretti Teatrali (foreground, right). In the distance we can make out the buildings of modern-day Pompeii.

**184-185** The town of Herculaneum was destroyed by the same eruption of Vesuvius (79 BC) that also annihilated Pompeii. So far the excavations of ancient Herculaneum have only succeeded in bringing to light the districts nearest to the sea. Several sites including the Forum, the temples, many houses, and the necropolis are still buried in part under the modern town of Resina.

**186-187** Inside the Archaeological Park of Pausilypon (Posillipo), near Naples, we find the lavish remains of the Vedio Pollione villa, built on a promontory found between the two Gaiola islets. The villa was commissioned in the 1st century BC by the wealthy knight Publius Vedius Pollio, and it comprises several buildings laid out around the domus: a large theater that was able to seat 2,000 spectators, a nymphaeum, the odeon, the belvedere and the upper and the lower spas.

**188** Paestum was founded by the Greeks in about 600 BC and was originally called Poseidonia, in honor of Poseidon (Neptune), the god of the sea to whom the city was dedicated. In 273 BC it became a Roman colony, named Paestum. The Heraion, the location of the temples shown here (dedicated to Hera, left and Neptune, right) was built was just outside the city at the port warehouses on the River Silaros.

**189** The Temple of Neptune (about 450 BC) is considered to be the best example of Doric architecture in Italy and also Greece. For centuries it was attributed to Neptune, in the belief that the most impressive building must have been built in honor of the god whose name had been given to the town. More recent research, however, attributes the temple to Apollo.

**190** In this image we are able to enjoy the perfect geometry of the temples of Paestum and to notice how much bigger the Temple of Neptune is compared to the temple dedicated to Hera. The image does not show Paestum's third great temple, which was dedicated to Ceres or Athena, and was built in about 500 BC.

**191** The temple of Hera was built in about 550 BC and dedicated to the bride of Zeus who was the main divinity of what was then called Poseidonia. It is not as high or as majestic as the Temple of Neptune, but it must have had very refined friezes, as proved by the numerous clay decoration elements found during excavation.

**192** The triumphal arch of Benevento was erected in AD 114 by the Roman senate and the people in order to honor the Emperor. The arch was part of the encircling walls and served as the entrance to the town from Via Traiana, the road that connected Rome to Brindisi.

**193** The River Sannio, the location of Maleventum, was a town that survived no less than three Roman wars and was the scene of the victory later achieved over Pirrus, King of Epirus. This victory and the definitive conquest of a strategic territory led the Romans to change the name of the city to Beneventum. An important crossroads in the direction of Apulia, Benevento became one of the Empire's most important cities. There are many remains dating back to the Roman domination, some very well preserved, like the Roman theater shown in the image.

**194** As an ally of Rome from the time of the Samnite wars, Lucera (Foggia) was a colony raised according to Latin law, in other words it was given independence, with its own magistrates and its own coinage, as well as various administrative privileges. The amphitheater, still well-preserved, dates back to the Imperial Age, the period when Lucera was at the height of its splendor.

**195** Venosa (Potenza) was conquered by the Romans at the end of the Samnite wars and, like Lucera, became a wealthy, flourishing colony. The town was dedicated to Venus and lay at the heart of a very fertile countryside, where precious vines were grown. Today's archeological park includes the baths, the amphitheater (in the image) and a religious complex, but only partly expresses the richness of this Via Appia village that turned into an important municipium.

**196 and 197** The Egnazia archeological site is in Apulia, midway between the regions of Bari and Salento. The site has one unique feature: part of the ruins are still covered by water, so it is not unusual for bathers and fishermen to bump into tombs cut into the rock or to find the remains of submerged temple columns. Egnazia is named for the temple of the nymph Egnathia, on whose altar those assigned to the cult would achieve the miracle of burning incense without the use of fire. Strabo and Horace were the first to describe Egnazia's long history, however its founders are still unknown to us but are likely to have come from the Aegean area.

**198** Lecce, probably of Greek origin, reached the peak of its splendor during the time of the Roman Empire. The best-preserved archeological relics date mainly to the era of Hadrian, when the city was called Licea. Worthy of note is the amphitheater, located in the city center, near the Piazza Sant'Oronzo. The monument's arena, its lower terraces and part of the outer walls are almost intact. Built in the 2nd century AD, it could seat over 25,000 spectators.

**200-201** Segesta, which was founded by the Elimians, who were refugees from Troy, was an important Hellenic center, linked closely to Athens. The theater, dated mid-3rd century BC, is the surviving proof of the city's heyday, and is set on the hillside opposite the temple, another of Segesta's great monuments. Dug partly into the rock, the theater could seat over 4,000 people.

**202 and 203 left** The great temple outside of Segesta's walls was never completed, in all likelihood because the city was taken by the Carthaginians in 409 BC. The general proportions and style features of the building are very much like those of the Classical architectural models found in Sicily's Greek towns, but we have no information about who was worshipped here.

**203 right** The theater, built on the north side of the Segesta acropolis, opens over a vast panorama that stretches from the Inici mountains down to the Gulf of Castellammare. The building was built of limestone blocks and in the typical Greek architectural style, but was a forerunner of Roman theater architecture solutions.

**204-205** Founded in about the mid-7th century BC by Greek settlers on Sicily's southwest coast, Selinunte was razed to the ground by the Carthaginians in 250 BC in order to stop the Romans from occupying it. The acropolis (in the image) is the oldest part of the city, which was built on a calcareous plateau. The monumental remains are visible, however, on the eastern and western slopes of the hills (the Fountain and the Malophoros Temple). The marvelous archeological park is completed by the remains of the necropolis and the city's port.

**206** The temple, identified with the letter E, stands on the east hill and can be dated to the mid-5th century BC. It is the best-preserved of the three temples visible on this side of Selinunte. An inscription revealed in a frieze and the presence of several identified metopes has led us to believe that the temple was originally dedicated to Hera.

**207** The other, now ruined, temples located on the east hill, known by the conventional letters F and G, were perhaps dedicated respectively to Athena and Zeus. Alongside temple E (bottom), temple F, which was the smallest (center), was plundered over the years and reduced to an open quarry for building materials; temple G, one of the biggest known in antiquity (top), dates back to the 5th century BC and was probably never finished.

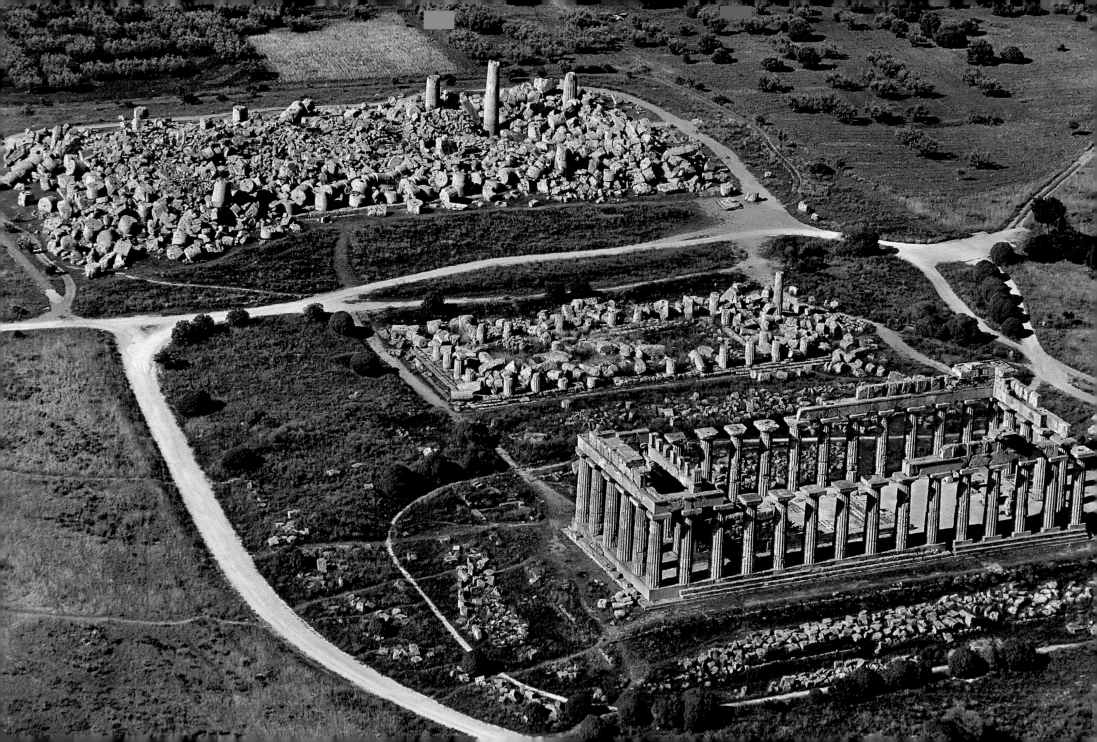

**208** The Temple of Hercules, dated to the 6th century BC, was destroyed by an earthquake. It is the oldest of those in Agrigento's Valley of the Temples. Hercules was deeply venerated in ancient Akragas where the "Eraclee" festival was dedicated to him.

**209** The Doric-style Temple of Concordia is the most impressive and best-preserved of the valley's monuments. It was built in the 5th century BC and transformed into a Christian basilica in AD 597.

**210-211** A long stretch of coast scattered with the remains of temples, altars and sanctuaries of the archaic age which was consecrated to Demetra, the goddess of fertility. The four surviving columns of the Temple of the Dioscuri soar in the center of the area.

**212** The Greek theater of Siracusa was built in the 5th century BC, on the slopes of the Temenite hill. It was practically rebuilt in the 3rd century BC and was further refurbished in the Roman era. Over the centuries it was plundered and used as a quarry, in particular by the Spanish, who erected their fortresses with the ready-cut stone blocks. Since 1914 the Istituto Nazionale del Dramma Antico has been organizing annual performances of Greek plays here.

**214** Catania's Roman theater is set against the hillside where the old acropolis stood: a site that has been embraced by the city over the centuries. The theater itself is now seamlessly enveloped between houses and lanes, and it was only modern-day excavations that freed it from more recent layers of development. In the past it could seat up to 7,000 spectators.

**215** The Roman amphitheater of Siracusa, built early in the Imperial period, is set in the area where the city's greatest number of ancient monuments are concentrated. Much of it was dug from the rock and it is a considerable size - over 460 ft. (140 m) long and 390 ft. (119 m) wide - making it the most majestic in Sicily.

**216-217** After Siracusa, the largest theater of Greek origin in Sicily is to be found in Taormina. Experts believe that it was built in the second half of the 3rd century BC, but remains found today refer to the new Roman building, which dates back to the period of Octavian Augustus (31 BC-AD 14).

**218-219** The Barumini complex was built with dry-stone walls, and includes circular truncated cone towers. It is the most complete example of Nuragic prehistoric architecture. The complex dates back to 1100 BC (Archaic Nuragic), but it was in use until Roman times (1st century BC).

**220 and 221** Historically, Nora is the oldest town to have been founded in Sardinia. Phoenician colonization, from the 8th century BC or thereabouts, made it into an important trade center with three ports, sadly none of which can be seen today. In the Punic period, Nora became one of the most important towns on the south coast of Sardinia; there are a few archaeological remains surviving from this period and they include the Temple of Tanit. Most remains can be dated back to the Roman domination, which began in 238 BC. Excavations have now brought to light vast areas of the Roman town, particularly from the Imperial period.

# Index

# Index

223

**Credits:**

**Antonio Attini/Archivio White Star:** pages 2-3, 4-5, 9, 12 left and right, 15, 20-21, 22-23, 24 left, 27, 28 center and right, 31, 33, 38, 39, 40-41, 42-43, 44, 45, 46-47, 50, 51, 54-55, 57, 60 right, 64, 66, 67, 72, 73 left and right, 75, 78 right, 82-83, 84, 85, 86, 87, 102-103, 109, 117, 124-125, 132-133, 135, 137, 139, 152 left, 153, 155, 156 center, 159, 168-169, 171, 174-175, 176, 177, 178, 179, 180, 181, 182, 183, 194, 195, 196, 197, 198, 200-201, 202, 203, 204-205, 206, 207, 208, 209, 210-211, 212, 214, 215, 216-217, 218-219, 220, 221
**BAMSphoto Rodella:** pages 28 left, 32, 48, 49
**Marcello Bertinetti/Archivio White Star:** pages 6-7, 8, 10, 12 center, 18-19, 25, 56, 59, 60 left, 60 center, 63, 76, 78 left, 79, 80, 88, 89, 90, 91, 91, 92, 93, 94, 95, 96-97, 98-99, 101, 104, 105, 106, 110, 111, 112, 113, 114, 118-119, 120, 121, 122, 123, 126, 128, 129, 130-131, 134, 136, 138, 141, 142, 143, 144, 145, 147, 148, 150-151, 152 right, 170, 188, 189, 190, 191
**Marcello Libra/Archivio White Star:** page 35
**Pubbli Aer Foto:** pages 52-53, 68, 69, 70-71
**Giulio Veggi/Archivio White Star:** pages 156 left and right, 161, 162, 163, 164, 165, 166, 167, 173, 184-185, 186-187, 192, 193
**IKONOS - image courtesy GeoEye - processing by WorldSat:** page 16
**Fabrizio Zani:** page 24 right

Photographs
**Antonio Attini**
**Marcello Bertinetti**

Text
**Enrico Lavagno**

Editor
**Valeria Manferto De Fabianis**

Editorial coordination
**Alberto Bertolazzi**
**Maria Valeria Urbani Grecchi**

The publisher would like to thank:
Stefano Travaglia, Mimmo Potenzieri, Roberto Barsotti, Paolo Barbieri,
Roberto Botti, Francesco Orrico, Walter Nasini, Avionord Milan, Star Fly srl
Rome, Werner Sailer, Associazione Aerostatica Toscana.
The publisher offers special thanks to Valentino Benvenuti, Elio Rullo, Emo,
Francesco and Fabio Bientinesi of Volitalia.

© 2007 White Star S.p.A.
Via Candido Sassone, 22/24
13100 Vercelli, Italy
www.whitestar.it

TRANSLATION: CHRISTINE RECCHIA

ISBN 978-88-544-0324-6

REPRINTS:
1 2 3 4 5 6   11 10 09 08 07

Color separation: Pixelab, Novara
Printed in China